For George Short

The Fossil Girl copyright © Frances Lincoln Limited 1999
Text and illustrations copyright © Catherine Brighton 1999
Back endpaper: *Mary Anning*, portrait by an unknown artist,
The Natural History Museum, London

First published in the United States in 1999 by
The Millbrook Press, 2 Old New Milford Road,
Brookfield, CT 06804

First published in Great Britain in 1999 by
Frances Lincoln Limited, 4 Torriano Mews
Torriano Avenue, London NW5 2RZ

Brighton, Catherine.
The fossil girl : Mary Anning's dinosaur discovery /
Catherine Brighton.
p. cm.
Summary: In simple cartoon style, tells the story of a twelve-year-
old English girl's discovery of an ichthyosaurus skeleton.
ISBN 0-7613-1468-7 (lib. bdg.)
1. Anning, Mary, 1799-1847—Juvenile literature. 2. Women
paleontologists—England— Biography—Juvenile literature.
3. Ichthyosaurus—Juvenile literature. [1. Anning. Mary,
1799-1847. 2. Paleontologists. 3. Women—Biography. 4. Cartoons
and comics.] I. Title
QE707.A56B75 1999
560'.92—dc21
[b]   98-36180
                                             CIP
                                             AC

Set in Gill Sans and Perpetua
Printed in Hong Kong
3 5 7 9 8 6 4 2

THE MILLBROOK PRESS   BROOKFIELD, CONNECTICUT

Catherine Brighton

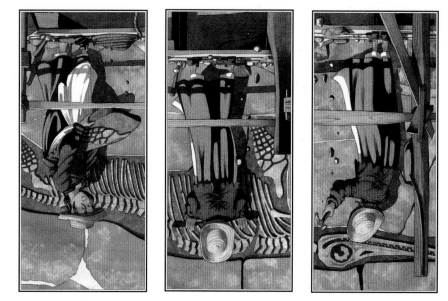

Mary Anning's Dinosaur Discovery

The FOSSIL GIRL

Lyme Regis, Dorset, England, 1810. Mary and Joe Anning went out in all weather to collect "curiosities" to sell in their shop. After their father died, they helped their mother keep the shop going.

Is it worth five shillings, Mama?

Yes, Mary. You write the label.

Before Mary went to bed, she watched the storm from the safety of the shop window.

And then suddenly, in the middle of the night, a huge wave burst through the windows, flooding the Annings' house.

All the curiosities were swept away.

Don't worry, Mama. Joe and I will soon find more curiosities. We'll start tomorrow.

Mr. Arkwright from up the hill
came to repair the damage.
Then Mary and Joe set out
to find some new curiosities.

That night, Mary lay awake thinking of a way to get her crocodile down from the cliff and into the shop.

Mary picked some flowers for Mr. Arkwright, and asked him if he would build her a tower up to the cliff. He was so intrigued, he said yes.

When the tower was ready, Mary climbed up the rickety ladder. The platform swayed under her. It was a long, long way down.

Then she turned to face the creature.

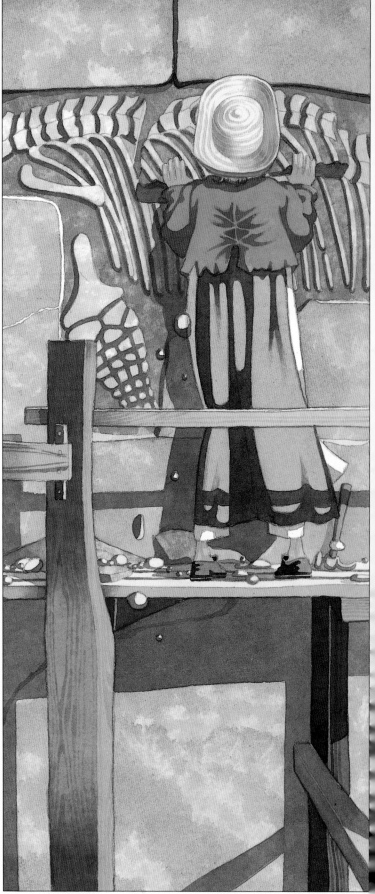

Mary lowered all the pieces into Mr. Arkwright's cart and took one last look at the hole where the curiosity had been buried all those years.

Well done, Mary!

When can we see the crocodile?

Bravo!

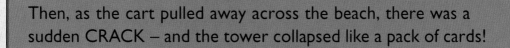

Then, as the cart pulled away across the beach, there was a sudden CRACK — and the tower collapsed like a pack of cards!

. . . while outside, a very long line was forming.

Mary and Joe charged each person a penny to see the curiosity.
Now they could afford their first hot meal for months.

Just when Mary and Joe thought the last sightseer had gone, a figure appeared at the door. It was Henry Henley, Lord of the Manor.

He was very interested to see the curiosity, and told them that the creature was not a crocodile . . .

These are the fossilized remains of what scientists call an Ichthyosaur. It lived in the sea millions of years ago. You've made a very, very important discovery.

Mary and Joe could hardly believe what he had told them.

So the world is millions of years old, Joe, not thousands!

And the creature has been in the cliff all that time!

Mary Anning did become famous.

After finding the Ichthyosaur, she went on to make many more important finds, including two complete Plesiosaurs and the first Pterodactyl ever found in Britain. Even though she never went to school and never left Lyme Regis, she made an international reputation as a fossil expert. She died in 1847 at the age of 48.

Mary lived at a time when scientists were working on a new idea — that the world was much older than they had always thought. This shocked some people, as it seemed to contradict what was written in the Bible. Mary's discoveries helped provide the evidence that the scientists needed to back up their new ideas.

In 1859, twelve years after Mary died, Charles Darwin's book The Origin of Species by Means of Natural Selection was published. His theory of evolution sparked off a revolution in religious and scientific thought, and its effects are still felt to this day.

Without Mary Anning and her fossils, the history of science might have been very different.